HAL•LEONARD®

VIOLIN PLAY-ALONG

AUDIO ACCESS INCLUDED

VOL. 69

LA LA LAND

MUSIC FROM THE MOTION PICTURE SOUNDTRACK

Jon Vriesacker, violin
Audio arrangements by Peter Deneff
Recorded and Produced by Jake Johnson
at Paradyme Productions

PLAYBACK+
Speed • Pitch • Balance • Loop

To access audio, visit:
www.halleonard.com/mylibrary

2300-1142-0848-7226

ISBN 978-1-4950-9273-2

Visit Hal Leonard Online at
www.halleonard.com

World headquarters, contact:
Hal Leonard
7777 West Bluemound Road
Milwaukee, WI 53213
Email: info@halleonard.com

In Europe, contact:
Hal Leonard Europe Limited
1 Red Place
London, W1K 6PL
Email: info@halleonardeurope.com

In Australia, contact:
Hal Leonard Australia Pty. Ltd.
4 Lentara Court
Cheltenham, Victoria, 3192 Australia
Email: info@halleonard.com.au

HAL•LEONARD®

VIOLIN PLAY-ALONG

AUDIO
ACCESS
INCLUDED

LA LA LAND

MUSIC FROM THE MOTION PICTURE SOUNDTRACK

Another Day of Sun

Music by Justin Hurwitz
Lyrics by Benj Pasek & Justin Paul

Someone in the Crowd

Music by Justin Hurwitz
Lyrics by Benj Pasek & Justin Paul

rall.

Slowly and freely

ff   *p*

Very slowly, in time

pp

accel. e cresc. poco a poco

Tempo I

f

ff

Mia & Sebastian's Theme

Music by Justin Hurwitz

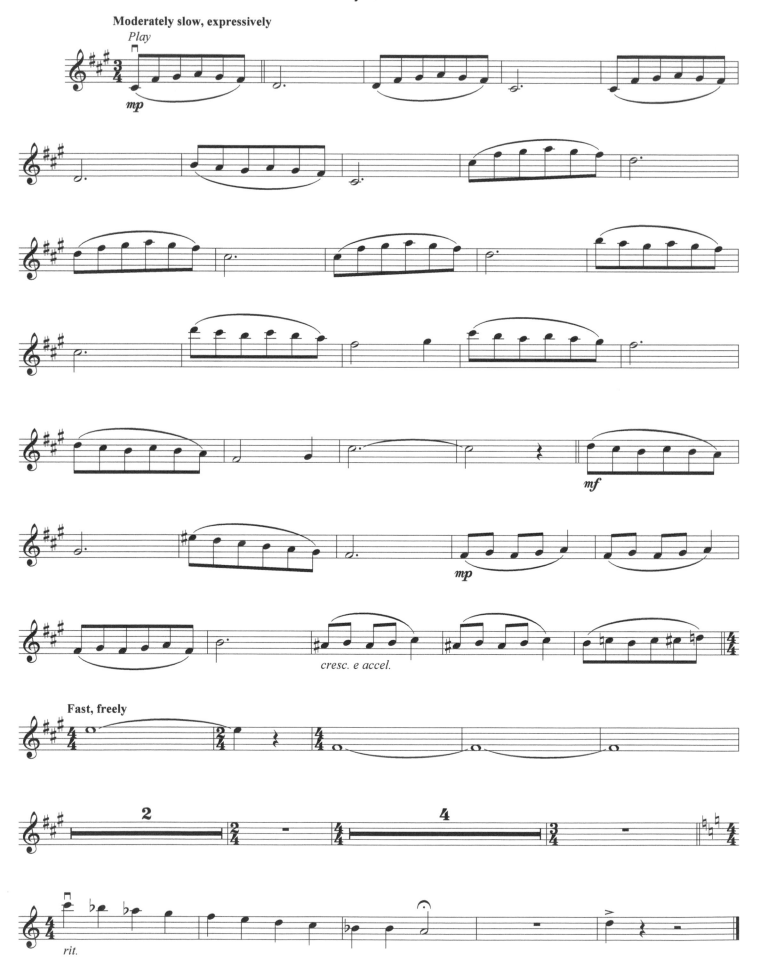

City of Stars

Music by Justin Hurwitz
Lyrics by Benj Pasek & Justin Paul

A Lovely Night

Music by Justin Hurwitz
Lyrics by Benj Pasek & Justin Paul

Planetarium

Music by Justin Hurwitz

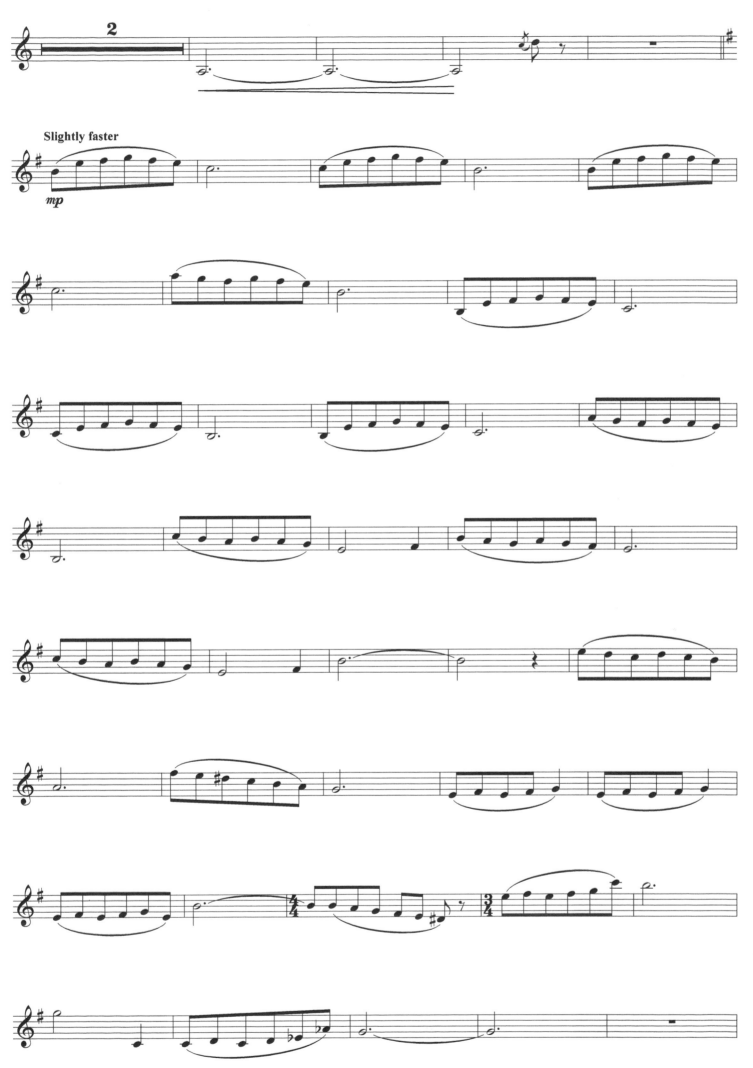

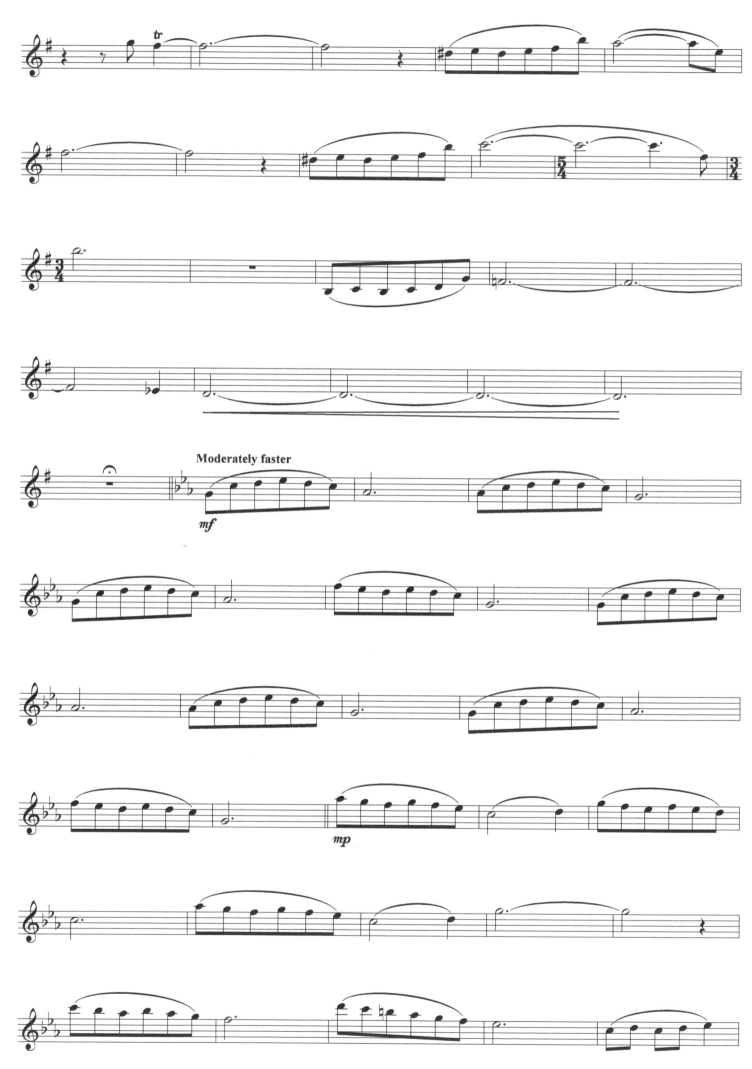

Start a Fire

Music & Lyrics by John Stephens, Angélique Cinélu, Marius De Vries and Justin Hurwitz

Audition
(The Fools Who Dream)

Music by Justin Hurwitz
Lyrics by Benj Pasek & Justin Paul